SOE: CHURCHILL'S SECRET AGENTS

Terry Crowdy

SHIRE PUBLICATIONS
Bloomsbury Publishing Plc

PO Box 883, Oxford, OX1 9PL, UK
1385 Broadway, 5th Floor, New York, NY 10018, USA
Email: shire@bloomsbury.com

SHIRE is a trademark of Osprey Publishing, a division
of Bloomsbury Publishing Plc

First published in Great Britain in 2016 by Shire
Publications

A CIP catalogue record for this book is available from
the British Library.

Shire Library no. 829.   ISBN-13: 978 1 78442 040 6

Terry Crowdy has asserted his right under the
Copyright, Designs and Patents Act, 1988, to be
identified as the author of this book.

Typeset in Garamond Pro and Gill Sans.

Printed in China through World Print Ltd.

19 20 21 22 23   10 9 8 7 6 5 4 3 2

www.shirebooks.co.uk
To find out more about our authors and books visit
our website. Here you will find extracts, author
interviews, details of forthcoming events and the
option to sign-up for our newsletter.

COVER IMAGE
Cover design by Peter Ashley, featuring a detail from
an English Heritage poster for 'Live and Let's Spy', an
exhibition mounted at Dover Castle in the mid-1990s,
celebrating the work of Charles Fraser-Smith. He
produced 'Q' devices for SOE operatives and is widely
acclaimed as the inspiration for Ian Fleming's character
'Q' in the James Bond novels. With grateful thanks
to the original photographer Carol Sharp and English
Heritage. Back cover: Detail of notebook on front cover.

TITLE PAGE IMAGE
Member of the French Resistance planting explosives
on a railway track. The disruption to rail traffic in
1944 slowed the movement of German reinforcements
to Normandy. (IWM HU 56936)

CONTENTS PAGE IMAGE
Dead rats were filled with explosives and left in
coal cellars; they would be shovelled into a boiler,
whereupon they would explode. (TNA HS 7/49)

IMAGE ACKNOWLEDGEMENTS
All of the images in this book are from the Imperial
War Museum or from The National Archives,
indicated in brackets at the end of each caption as
'IWM' or 'TNA' respectively.

IMPERIAL WAR MUSEUM COLLECTIONS
IWM (Imperial War Museums) is a global authority on
conflict and its impact, from the First World War to the
present day, in Britain, its Empire and Commonwealth.
Founded in 1917 when the First World War was still
being fought, IWM collects material that records
people's experiences of modern war. The collections
include everyday objects such as uniform, clothing,
mementoes or household items, whereas other objects
testify to the most extraordinary events of modern
times. Together, they tell of human spirit and resilience,
creation and destruction, lives torn apart or brought
back together. Our evolving collections reveal stories of
people, places, ideas and events. They will change the
way you think about war. iwm.org.uk

THE NATIONAL ARCHIVES
The National Archives is the UK government's official
archive containing over 1,000 years of history. They
give detailed guidance to government departments
and the public sector on information management, and
advise other about the care of historical archives.

Shire Publications supports the Woodland Trust, the UK's leading woodland conservation charity. Between 2014 and 2018 our donations are being
spent on their Centenary Woods project in the UK.

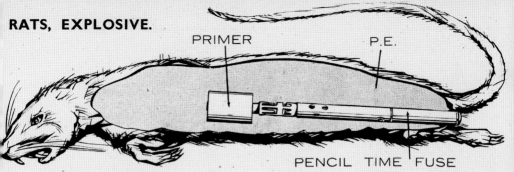

RATS, EXPLOSIVE.

PRIMER

P.E.

PENCIL TIME FUSE

A rat is skinned, the skin being sewn up and filled with P.E. to assume the shape of a dead rat. A Standard No. 6 Primer is set in the P.E. Initiation is by means of a short length of safety fuse with a No. 27 detonator crimped on one end, and a copper tube igniter on the other end, or, as in the case of the illustration above, a P.T.F. with a No. 27 detonator attached. The rat is then left amongst the coal beside a boiler and the flames initiate the safety fuze when the rat is thrown on to the

CONTENTS

SET EUROPE ABLAZE

THE SPECIAL OPERATIONS Executive was one of the most innovative British creations of the Second World War. Its mission was to export resistance and subversion, and to undertake sabotage in occupied Europe and beyond, disrupting the Axis war effort through direct attacks and building so-called 'secret armies', which would rise up in support of conventional Allied forces at the appropriate time. Potential agents were carefully selected and put through intensive paramilitary and parachute training, then taught how to live clandestinely behind enemy lines, to operate radio sets and write in codes. In secret research stations, the implements of sabotage and assassination were designed and manufactured; everything from silent pistols to submersible canoes.

Prior to the Second World War, the United Kingdom had two secret services, neither of which was publicly acknowledged until 1992. Both agencies had their roots in a Secret Service Bureau established in 1909. The agency responsible for counterespionage within the territories of the British Empire was the Security Service, MI5. Although the title of the agency suggests it formed part of a 'Military Intelligence' service, it was in fact controlled by the Home Office. The agency responsible for gathering secret intelligence about foreign powers was known as MI6. This organisation was part of the Foreign Office and was (still is) more properly titled the Secret Intelligence Service (SIS). The title MI6 was used by the service as a 'flag of convenience', because it

Opposite: B-17G Flying Fortresses drop containers to the French Resistance. Precision flying was required: too high and the containers would be scattered; too low and they might break on impact. (IWM EA 34185)

suggested there was an organisational link with MI5. Within SIS was an autonomous signals intelligence organisation known as the Government Code and Cypher School (GCCS). This organisation was responsible for providing secure communications for British officials, and studying the encryption methods of foreign powers. It would go on to achieve great acclaim for its activities at Bletchley Park.

Neither MI5 nor MI6 had a remit to undertake sabotage activities or promote subversion in foreign countries. The Spanish Civil War (1936–9) and the Munich Crisis of 1938 showed the potential power of so-called 'fifth columnists' – agents working openly or covertly to undermine from within a country on behalf of a belligerent power. While MI5 looked towards preventing potential fifth column activities at home, in 1938 SIS formed a D Section under Major Lawrence Grand. The section (allegedly 'D' for 'destruction') examined staging possible fifth column

The Fairbairn-Sykes 'FS' double-edged fighting knife produced by Wilkinson and Sword. With hilt the dagger was 29cm in length and made of steel. (IWM WEA 4166)

activities within Germany, including sabotage operations and cooperation with internal groups opposed to the Nazis.

At the time there was a great deal of misgiving about undertaking these operations. SIS was at heart an intelligence-gathering organisation. It gathered secrets by identifying sources, usually people with access to state secrets and a grudge or an exploitable character trait, and inducing them to betray these secrets for various incentives. Intelligence gathering was a methodical and stealthy process, usually undertaken by SIS officers working undercover in embassies or consulates, and did not often involve the sort of daring escapades now attributed to fictional spies. If British agents were to begin running amok in Europe, blowing things up, it was feared the ensuing security clampdowns would hinder its core intelligence-gathering mission.

At the same time D Section was created, a small War Office research section called MI(R) was formed. Led by

An RAF Lysander Mark IIIA of No. 161 (Special Duties) Squadron. This aircraft flew twenty missions into occupied France, delivering and collecting SOE and French Resistance personnel. (IWM HU 59359)

Lieutenant Colonel 'Jo' Holland, at the end of 1938 MI(R) began to study irregular warfare. It drew on the experiences of the Anglo-Irish War (1919–21) and the exploits of T. E. Lawrence leading Arab irregulars against the Ottoman forces in the Great War. Studies were also made of the tactics of the Boers, Bolsheviks, and the belligerents in Palestine during the Arab Revolt (1936–9). In addition to Holland's work, Major Millis Jefferis set up a secret workshop which began to develop sabotage equipment such as time-fuses and limpet bombs. By the spring of 1939 MI(R) and D Section were actively cooperating. In May that year handbooks were published on the art of guerrilla warfare, advice to partisan leaders, and how to use high explosives.

The aftermath of a Polish resistance attack on a German military train in April 1944. (TNA HS 7/185/32)

Following the 1940 Nazi offensive in Western Europe there was a move to unite D Section and MI(R). There naturally followed a bout of political lobbying over which government department should control the new body.

The front-runners were the War Office, thus linking the objectives with those of the Armed Forces, and the Foreign Office, thus linking it with SIS. In fact SOE went to neither. The Special Operations Executive was created on 22 July 1940, forming a department within the Ministry of Economic Warfare (MEW). This Ministry had been created in September 1939 and was charged with forming an economic blockade of Germany by denying the Nazis access to markets and strategic raw materials. When planning an economic blockade, it was recognised that sabotage and stirring unrest among a foreign labour force might also prove useful. The Minister of Economic Warfare, Hugh Dalton, was ultimately successful in persuading Churchill he should have control over SOE to help him achieve his department's wider objectives. In giving Dalton control of the new department, Churchill famously instructed him to 'set Europe ablaze'.

Station XVb – SOE's 'Demonstration Room' at the Natural History Museum was a 'must see' experience for senior Allied leaders, including King George VI. (TNA HS 10/1/3)

ORGANISATION

THROUGHOUT THE WAR SOE operated under the cover title Inter Services Research Bureau (ISRB). Its headquarters were well away from the Whitehall hub of government, at 64 Baker Street, London. The association with Sherlock Holmes (fictionally at 221b Baker Street) led to SOE being nicknamed 'the Baker Street Irregulars'. At the end of October 1944 SOE reached its peak with almost 13,000 staff on the books. Of these approximately one fifth were of officer rank, and the majority (9,000) were drawn from the armed forces. Women accounted for 3,200 members, 400 of whom had officer status.

When first formed, SOE comprised three groups: SO1 Propaganda, SO2 Operations, and SO3 Research. The first group had been created from a secret 'black propaganda' organisation known as EH, after its first headquarters at Electra House in London. In August 1941 SO1 went on to form a separate entity, the Political Warfare Executive (PWE) and therefore falls outside this account. Little is remembered of SO3 in the official history of SOE. The former SOE employee and Soviet spy, Kim Philby, recorded in his memoirs it soon 'drowned in paperwork of its own creating'. The Operations group SO2 went on to become SOE as history now records it.

The organisation was managed by a council composed of sixteen members – a mixture of directorate heads and advisers. This was led by the Chief of the Organisation &

Opposite: The interior of Station VIIa, the wireless production factory at Bontex Knitting Mill, Beresford Avenue, Wembley. (IWM HU 56752)

Chairman of Council (a role abbreviated to CD, the former designation of Chief of Section D). Three men held this post. The first Director of SOE was Sir Frank Nelson. His successor in 1942 was Sir Charles Hambro, from Hambros Bank which specialised in Scandinavian business. The last, in September 1943, was Major-General Colin Gubbins, who had been SOE's Director of Operations and Training since October 1940. Prior to joining SOE, Gubbins was an expert in guerrilla warfare, and had set up the secret Auxiliary Units in 1940 – a British resistance force if the Nazis had invaded.

By 1944 operations were managed by three regional directorates. The London Group covered Western Europe, Germany and Scandinavia. This directorate was composed of various Country Sections responsible for operations. France had up to nine different Country Sections, the main ones being F Section (independently British led) and RF

The Minister of Economic Warfare, Hugh Dalton (right) and SOE's Director of Operations and Training, Colin Gubbins (second right) talking to Czech officers. (IWM H 8185)

(managed in conjunction with de Gaulle's Free French). In the field, agents would form a network or 'circuit' centred on an organiser backed by radio operators and couriers. The Mediterranean Operations directorate had its headquarters in Cairo and covered the Western Mediterranean, Italy, the Balkans and Central Europe. Thirdly, Operations Far East & Missions covered South East Asia, Australia and Africa, as well as liaison with the USA and Soviet Union. The South East Asia component began as an 'India Mission' at Meerut, initially operating under the name of GSI(k) – a record keeping section within General Headquarters (GHQ) India. In December 1944 the organisation moved to Ceylon (Sri Lanka) in order to cooperate more closely with the Allied South East Asia Command (SEAC). From this point on, SOE used the designation Force 136.

The Plasterer's Shop where ingenious hiding places were created. One of the more exotic schemes saw camel dung collected from London Zoo for use as a model. (TNA HS 7/49)

Silence is of the Gods
...only monkeys chatter

The Property Shop at Station XV. Technicians would use sandpaper and Vaseline to age the suitcases used for hiding radio sets so they did not stand out. (TNA HS 7/49)

Under the Supplies directorate SOE also maintained a large number of research and supply facilities around the UK. The Research Section maintained a network of workshops, which sourced or built everything a secret agent required. Working under the ISRB cover name this section was staffed by specialists from industry, academia and the armed forces. The team at Station IX (the Frythe, Welwyn Garden City) produced everything from time-fuses, explosive and incendiary devices to poisons. The engineering team designed special firearms such as silenced pistols, concealable 'sleeve-guns' (see page 58–9), and even a miniature gun hidden in a woodbine cigarette. Perhaps overstepping SOE's operational requirements, they also designed and built midget submarines and freighters, and submersible canoes; anything the boffins anticipated the agents on mission might require. Station XV (the Thatched Barn) became the main production centre for the Camouflage Section. Largely staffed by film industry technicians, this team provided everything from civilian clothing to visual disguises for the agents, and the means of concealing everything from a radio set to a box of grenades. They employed European tailors and methods to ensure clothes did not exhibit obviously British designs. There was a Documents Section at Station XIV (Briggens at Roydon in Essex) which supplied SOE with all its forgery needs.

Initially SOE was reliant on SIS for its signalling requirements, but from 1 June 1942 it was free to produce its own radios and codes. The Signals Directorate became one of the largest in SOE with staff employed in the development of new radios, as wireless operators and coders. In addition to SOE's main wireless stations at Grendon and Poundon in Buckinghamshire, there were additional Main Stations in Cairo, Algeria, Freetown, Lagos, and Durban, as well as in India, Ceylon and Australia.

The main base of SOE's Camouflage Section was Station XV, the Thatched Barn on the Barnet bypass at Borehamwood, Hertfordshire (now, sadly, demolished). (TNA HS 7/49)

LESSONS IN UNGENTLEMANLY WARFARE

As a secret organisation, SOE could not openly advertise for recruits, so candidates were normally selected on an invitation-only basis. Initially the candidates were the likes of businessmen, engineers, or journalists with experience in working abroad. Preference was also given to those of dual nationality and possessing the requisite language skills or knowledge of the target area. Soldiers with similar skills were also invited to join, and in time, the various Country Sections selected their own agents from refugees from the occupied territories or the colonies. With candidates coming from such a wide variety of backgrounds and being recruited for many different purposes, it is difficult to generalise, but to best illustrate the process of recruitment and training when SOE was at its height, we might follow a typical agent recruited to SOE's French F section.

If the candidate was a civilian, their first contact with SOE might be a letter requesting they come for an interview on some war-related matter. Interviews for F Section were mostly held at the former Hotel Victoria on Northumberland Avenue, just a short walk from the War Office. In this requisitioned building (known then as Northumberland House) was a sparsely furnished room where the candidate would be sized up by Major Selwyn Jepson, who had been a detective author and screenwriter before the war. Conversation would flip between French and English, with Jepson probing the candidate's suitability for secret work, without actually giving details.

While the candidate privately conjectured on the purpose of the interview, Jepson weighed up if the interviewee was unduly rash, imprudent, or if they were suitably motivated, sound of mind and physically capable of the mission ahead. If this first meeting was a success, the candidate would be invited back for several more interviews. During these Jepson would explain the work was secret, might involve travel to occupied Europe, and that there was a high degree of risk involved, but no specifics would yet be mentioned.

Training on a firing range with a succession of pop-up targets activated by watching instructors. The agent holds his Sten Gun like a rifle for greater accuracy. (IWM MH 24447)

Having completed the interview stage, prospective agents were put through a series of 'schools'. SOE's training course had been drawn up by Major F. T. Davies in 1940 and was divided into four groups:

1. Preliminary schools
2. Paramilitary schools (known as Group A)
3. Finishing schools (known as Group B)
4. Country Section briefing and despatch

Students learn the Fairbairn-Sykes pistol shooting method. From a crouched position they were taught to instinctively point the pistol at the target rather than wasting time to aim. (IWM MH 24450)

The students (as the candidates were now termed) were guided through the groups by a series of conducting officers, many of whom were active or former agents recuperating from missions. While encouraging and coaching the students, the conducting officers also monitored their suitability, and reported any negative traits that might not have come out during the interview stage. At every stage students were given the opportunity to drop out. Unsuccessful students would be sent into a form of quarantine known as 'the Cooler' in Inverness-shire so they did not disclose secrets that might jeopardise their fellow students.

The first stage was preliminary school. These schools were established in a series of large houses in the Home Counties known as Special Training Schools (STS). Here the agents went through a series of tests and assessments to confirm they were suitable for the more rigorous training ahead. Even at this stage nothing was said about the ultimate purpose of their training. F Section students were initially sent to STS4, Wanborough Manor near Guildford. As SOE became more experienced in the selection of agents, in June 1943 STS7

Sabotage demonstration against electricity transformers. Before embarking on a mission, agents would learn how to inflict maximum damage on plant and equipment. (IWM MH 24430)

(Winterfold House, Cranleigh) was opened, and a new Student Assessment Board created to administer a series of psychological and practical tests.

If suitable, students were then sent to the Group A schools for their paramilitary training. These were based in

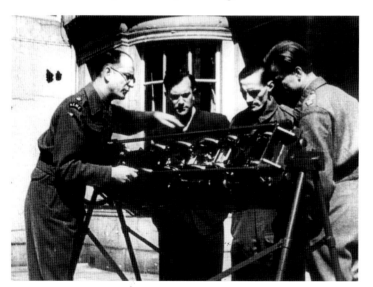

A group of students is instructed in sabotage against steam locomotives. It was important to target components that were the most difficult for the enemy to replace. (IWM MH 24439)

Students are taught rail demolition on sections of track in the Western Highlands of Scotland. (IWM MH 24449)

a series of shooting lodges around Arisaig and Morar in the Western Highlands where, in the spring of 1940, MI(R) had established a commando training centre. Here the students were subjected to three to five weeks of gruelling lessons. Combat training was unorthodox by regular army standards, and was the forerunner of modern Special Forces techniques. Students were taught the art of silent killing, using knives and unarmed combat. Rather than standard military pistol training, where the shooter was taught to aim using a straight arm, students learnt the technique of 'instinctive shooting', crouching like a boxer and firing from the hip at close range. The style owed more to gangster combat, and was developed by William Fairbairn and Eric Sykes, a pair of former Shanghai riot policemen who had vast experience with close combat. Fairbairn was a martial arts expert skilled in the use of knives; Sykes was a firearms expert who developed the technique of always shooting a target twice in quick succession. In his experience, an assailant high on adrenaline might survive a single shot and return fire, or throw a grenade. However, the body was less able to withstand the shock of two or more hits in quick succession. This Special Forces technique survives to the present day and is known as 'the double tap'.

Students would also go for long hikes in the mountains (hill walking was said to strengthen the ankles – useful for

parachutists) where they also practised orienteering and field craft. They would also be taught the Morse code and the rudiments of sabotage, using explosives for demolition work.

Having completed the paramilitary course, students would be sent to No. 1 Parachute Training School, RAF Ringway, Cheshire (now Manchester Airport). Kept segregated from other users of the school in nearby safe houses, SOE trainees would spend several days practising on harness swings, and landing on crash mats. They would then travel to nearby Tatton Park to make four jumps, the first from tethered balloons at a height of 700 feet (real mission jumps could be from as low as 300 feet) and then from aircraft. On completion of their fifth jump (this was usually the operational mission jump), agents were awarded their parachutist wings badge. Female agents completed only three training jumps, and therefore did not qualify for their 'parachute wings', a source of great injustice to many.

The Group B Finishing Schools were located on the Montagu Estate at Beaulieu in Hampshire. Students here were subjected to a three-week course which was structured in five departments:

1. Technique of clandestine existence
2. Practical exercises in clandestine living

Above left: SOE students at Beaulieu are lectured in the structure of resistance cells and security. (IWM MH 24438)

Above: Lessons in communicating with aircraft using a Eureka/ Rebecca navigation system. The ground equipment was a beacon to guide pilots to the drop zone. (IWM MH 24442)

3. Enemy organisation
4. Propaganda
5. Codes

When posing as a civilian in occupied Europe, agents required cover stories to explain their sudden appearance in society – preferably ones that could not be easily traced by the local authorities. Since being occupied by the Nazis, the daily life of civilians had changed significantly, with new official papers, ration cards and so on, all of which might come as a surprise to the newly arrived agent. Language skills were therefore only part of the knowledge an agent needed to possess. SOE had to fill in the gaps on life in the occupied territories as best it could, based on intelligence gained from refugees, escaped servicemen, returning agents and other sources. Having been established after the fall of France, SOE was handicapped by not having established networks of agents already in Europe. When the Soviet Union entered the war in 1941 the NKVD (forerunner of the KGB) profited from a pre-existing cadre of communist agents across Europe. The first SOE agents therefore had to go into the occupied territories blind, and so students had to be taught how to build up their own networks, recruiting agents, forming them into cells and establishing security to protect these cells if one was captured or betrayed. Basic agent field craft techniques like using elaborate passwords, 'cut outs' (intermediaries who could pass messages between agents and sources) and 'dead drops' (places where messages could be hidden) were extremely important.

Parachute training at RAF Ringway. Here students practise how to roll on landing having descended the slide. (IWM MH 24444)

SOE's Textile Shop. Up to sixteen agents could be fitted out each day by tailors who copied the latest Continental designs. (TNA HS 7/49)

In order to promote their cause and attract recruits, the students were given lessons in propaganda. The syllabus for this course was developed by Kim Philby who, unknown to his colleagues, was also a Soviet spy. An interesting feature of the Finishing School was the teaching of the criminal arts. Students were given masterclasses in lock picking and burglary; they were taught how to climb drainpipes and smash windows silently, how to break into safes, and how to make casts of keys. They were shown how to create disguises and, in extreme circumstances, SOE had access to plastic surgeons who could change the appearance of an agent who was perhaps too well known in the occupied territories.

SOE Camouflage Section could provide an agent with a complete new look. In some cases plastic surgery might be used, or even skin dyes. (TNA HS 7/49/142)

Clandestine communication was another key skill, so students were taught cryptology. Codes were initially very simple and based on poems. The agent was asked to remember a poem and then select certain words from it for each message. Each letter in the word was given a number and this was used to form a key. For example if the words 'bluebirds', 'white' and 'Dover' were selected, the agent would assign each letter a number based on its position in the

alphabet. If a letter was used more than once, they would be numbered in order from left to right. For example:

B	L	U	E	B	I	R	D	S	W	H	I	T	E	D	O	V	E	R
1	11	17	5	2	9	13	3	15	19	8	10	16	6	4	12	18	7	14

The agent would next write out his message in a grid, with the table numbered as above.

1	11	17	5	2	9	13	3	15	19	8	10	16	6	4	12	18	7	14
S	U	P	P	L	Y	D	R	O	P	R	E	Q	U	I	R	E	D	A
T	N	E	X	T	F	U	L	L	M	O	O	N	S	T	E	N	S	A
M	M	O	G	R	E	N	A	D	E	S	M	O	N	E	Y	T	O	O

Reading vertically, the column labelled 1 is STM; 2 is LTR; 3 is RLA, and so on. The letters would be put into groups of five letters for ease of sending, with random letters inserted to make up the final group. The message would therefore be received in London as:

STMLT RRLAI TEPXG USNDS OROSY FEEOM
UNMRE YDUNA AOOLD QNOPE OENTP MEOED

This was a fairly simple process to remember, but it was not very secure. The Germans were able to intercept messages being broadcast from England, and so could identify all the messages attributed to a particular agent's call sign. If the poem was not very long, or was something obvious, like the Lord's Prayer, or the national anthem, German cryptographers would quickly break the code. Once the poem was revealed, all the agent's back traffic could also be broken. SOE's chief cryptographer, Leo Marks, was appalled at the simplicity of the system. He composed original poems for agents so at least it was more

difficult for the Germans to guess the content.

He also set about developing new solutions, including 'worked out key' (WOK) one-time pads, where the agent was given a book of codes which were used only once and then discarded.

Once the elements of field craft had been gleaned, students were sent on training missions somewhere in Britain. This might be to spy on an industrial plant or to follow someone. Each of the students was issued with a letter to give to the police if they were arrested and questioned. Students might also be subjected to mock interrogations designed to prepare them for the ordeal of being questioned by the Nazi or Quisling security services. Through this training, it was emphasised that the agent had to hold out long enough for their capture to become known, and to give the others at least twenty-four hours to escape. If their initial cover story failed, they could

Welrod silenced pistol developed by SOE's Station IX (the 'Wel' stood for Welwyn). The pistol had a range of 8 yards. This example fired a 9 mm Parabellum round.
(IWM FIR 3801)

ABRASIVE POWDER

Catalogue No. HS 77c.

DESCRIPTION.

A fine carborundum powder, which is grey in colour and crystalline in substance.

METHOD OF USE.

Mix with the lubricating oil, or throw in dry if parts are exposed.

DIMENSIONS.

Height 2⅜".   Width 2¼".
Thickness 1¼".

WEIGHT. 3 oz. per tin.

PACKING AND SPECIAL NOTES.

As required.

Abrasive powder was a fine carborundum powder, which was mixed into lubricating oil. When the oil was applied to machinery it would foul up moving mechanical parts.
(TNA HS 7/28)

PLASTER LOGS.

A range of plaster logs designed for shipping arms and ammunition. The arms are packed in cardboard containers and sealed to protect from damp. They are then built into dummy logs made of plaster, which are modelled on actual types of trees common to the countries to which the shipments are being made. The plaster is then painted and garnished with moss, green lichen, or other tree fungi.

Wooden logs with a hollow cavity in the centre are also used for concealment of stores and ammunition. See illustration below.

Hollow plaster logs made excellent hiding places for grenades and other munitions. (TNA HS 7/49)

always fall back on claiming they were black marketeers, or even downed airmen. If they fell into the hands of the Gestapo (Nazi secret police), the interrogation was likely to be a brutal ordeal of beatings, electrocutions, and water torture. It was probably at this point in the training they were told about the 'L' pills – lethal cyanide capsules issued to each agent to spare them the ordeal of torture.

After graduating from the Group B schools, the student might then receive mission-specific training at one of SOE's many Special Training Schools. The Training School at Brickendonbury near Hertford (STS 17) was SOE's industrial sabotage school. Here the syllabus concentrated on identifying the most critical target in an industrial process and then providing exactly the right quantity of explosive required to put it out of action. For example, rather than breaking into a heavily guarded factory, it might be more productive to target its power plant. A well-conceived and delivered act of sabotage could achieve a level of precision far beyond the capabilities of strategic area bombing.

Radio operators were taught codes and ciphers over a six-week course which included fourteen days' security training. It was vital for the security of the team that the circuit organiser and radio operator kept apart. It was also important that the

When agents finished their training they were handed over to the Country Sections for mission briefings. Here a model is used to familiarise the agents with the target area. (IWM MH 24448)

radio operator moved around, transmitting from different locations to avoid detection. A classic tactic was for the Germans to switch off the power in a particular district and if the radio suddenly stopped transmitting, they knew where to search. Some SOE agents attempted to circumvent this control by wiring their sets to car batteries. Of course, radio operators were at their most vulnerable while moving with their cumbersome radio sets and ran the risk of being stopped at checkpoints or by enemy patrols. Once the syllabus was mastered, radio operators were allowed to practise clandestine broadcasts in England, with Scotland Yard and local police services acting as hostile interceptors. The course was extremely demanding, and even at full capacity only sixteen to eighteen operators a month were produced.

Certain Country Sections established their own specialist schools. By 1943 the Poles and Czechs assumed responsibility for training their own agents. The overseas branches of SOE developed their own training schools. For example, in the Middle East SOE used RAF Ramat David near Haifa (then Palestine) for parachute training. The facilities here were not to the same standard as RAF Ringway, and SOE trainees would practise their landing rolls by jumping from the back of a moving lorry onto sand.

PARACHUTIST, SUITS (STRIPTEASE SUITS)

Catalogue No. 22C/733 (Size 1). **22C/734** (Size 2)
22C/735 (Size 3). **22C/736** (Size 4).

GLOVES, GAUNTLET

GLOVES, LININGS, SILK

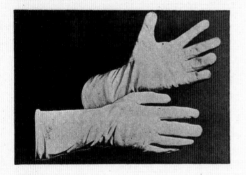

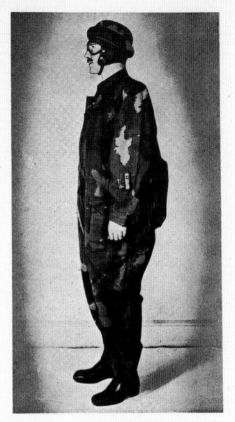

DESCRIPTION. These are made of either white or camouflaged canvas in four sizes. A zip fastener on each side is fitted for rapid exit from the suit, and these fasteners can be operated in either direction. A fly zip is also provided. On the left hip, is an external pocket for pistol and on the inside is a felt lined pocket designed to fit the spade, parachutist. Slightly to the rear of this pocket is a long narrow pocket for the spade handle.

At the lower outside edge of the left sleeve is a pocket for dagger or fighting knife and under each armpit, also outside, is a further pocket large enough to hold a second pistol, or emergency rations, etc. One large and one smaller pocket is fitted inside on the right.

A large pocket is provided to receive the spine pad, if used. This pocket is large enough to hold a brief case. At the neck is a leather strap to which is attached the helmet. All pockets have press stud fasteners.

The suits are large enough to permit of the wearing of two greatcoats if desired.

Flying Gauntlets with silk linings and Waistcoats, life saving, can also be used with these suits if required, in which case the standard R.A.F. pattern is provided.

DIMENSIONS.		WEIGHT
Size 1 - Up to 5 ft. 4 ins.		
,, 2 - From 5 ft. 4 ins. to 5 ft. 8 ins.		
,, 3 - From 5 ft. 8 ins. to 5 ft. 11 ins.		4½ lbs.
,, 4 - From 5 ft. 11 ins. to 6 ft. 4 ins.		

PARACHUTISTS, HELMETS

Catalogue No. 22C/965 (Size 1). **22C/966** (Size 2). **22C/967** (Size 3). **22C/968** (Size 4).

DESCRIPTION. Made of similar material to the suits, parachutist and in the same colours. There are four sizes all fitted with mica goggles fastened

OPERATIONS

IN A PAPER dated 21 May 1941 Gubbins outlined a three-stage plan for SOE operations. The first stage was to organise and equip a 'sabotage system' in the occupied territories. Next would come the building of 'underground armies' and providing them with organisation and training. Lastly would come the revolt stage, which would only be successful if sufficient airborne troops could be landed in support, along with the required supplies. Gubbins firmly believed resisters should never become involved in a pitched battle and should avoid being pinned down in a battle where the enemy could deploy superior forces and armament. In the first case, sabotage missions could be performed by teams infiltrated for the specific purpose, after which they might leave. The formation of 'secret armies' was a much longer-term proposition which required agents to remain in the occupied territories for extended periods.

A classic targeted mission was the 1942 Operation *Anthropoid*. Following the Munich Agreement of September 1938, the Nazi Reich had absorbed the Czech regions of Bohemia and Moravia. The political nature of the occupation meant there was no armed resistance to the Nazis as was the case in Poland and other countries invaded after 1939. Moreover, the industrial output of the country was a key asset to the Nazi war machine, and in the early part of the war the distant Czech armament factories were extremely difficult targets for the RAF. The Czech government in exile

Opposite: A parachutist's 'striptease' suit. This was a disposable camouflage overall which protected the agent's civilian clothes when jumping from an aircraft. (TNA HS 7/28)

Heydrich's Mercedes-Benz 320 Cabriolet in Klein Holeschow-itzerstrasse after the attack. The grenade exploded outside the vehicle by the damaged door. (IWM HU 47379)

decided there should be some demonstration of resistance to Nazi occupation and so ordered the assassination of Nazi *Reichsprotektor* of Bohemia and Moravia, Reinhard Heydrich.

SOE trained two agents for the mission: the Czech, Jan Kubiš and the Slovak, Jozef Gabčík, then infiltrated them into the country. On the morning of 27 May 1942 Heydrich left his home for Prague Castle riding in an open top car. Kubiš and Gabčík positioned themselves at a tram stop by a sharp bend in the road where Heydrich's driver would have to slow down. An accomplice was positioned further up the road to alert the two agents Heydrich was approaching. Everything appeared to be going to plan. As the vehicle slowed, Gabčík stepped in front of the car armed with a Sten gun, took aim and fired. The weapon jammed. Rather than speeding off, Heydrich ordered his driver to stop and drew a pistol to shoot at Gabčík. At this point Kubiš threw a grenade at the car but it fell short. Heydrich and Kubiš were both struck by shrapnel but continued to fight, all three men now exchanging pistol fire. When it appeared the attempt had failed, Kubiš escaped on a bicycle while Gabčík ran on foot. At last realising he had been wounded by the grenade, Heydrich ordered his chauffeur to give chase on foot, but Gabčík wounded the German with two pistol shots. Initially the agents believed their attack had failed, but fragments of the grenade and vehicle upholstery had entered Heydrich's body. He died from infection on 4 June 1942.

Although Heydrich had been targeted because of his role as *Reichsprotektor*, he was a senior member of the Nazi elite, and was head of the SS intelligence service (RSHA). The Nazi response to his assassination was swift and violent. Thousands of troops poured into Prague and began a manhunt. On 10 June, the day after Heydrich's funeral, the village of Lidice was destroyed, its men massacred and women and children sent to concentration camps. It was claimed Lidice had given shelter to the partisans carrying out the attack. On 17 June the agents' hiding place in the Church of Saints Cyril and Methodius in Prague was revealed. The next morning hundreds of Waffen-SS troops laid siege to the church and a ferocious gun battle broke out. Kubiš and two accomplices were killed in the prayer loft, while Gabčík and three others committed suicide in the crypt to avoid capture.

Although the cost in terms of reprisals was prohibitive, the fact such a leading Nazi could be targeted and killed showed SOE could play an important part in the war effort. However, perhaps because of the reprisals, assassinations were very much the exception to the rule. In 1944 SOE

Heydrich's death reported on 15 June 1942 in the Nazi Interior Ministry newspaper *Die Deutsche Polizei*. The assassination of Heydrich showed that even the highest ranking Nazis were not untouchable. (TNA WO 208/4472/4)

A 3-pound charge of plastic explosive (PE) attached by cordtex detonating cord. One of the advantages of PE was that it could be cut and shaped as required. (TNA HS 7/28)

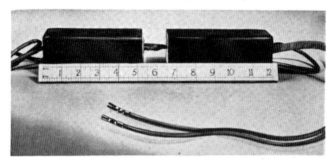

STANDARD CHARGE, 3 LB., SPLIT

contemplated assassinating Adolf Hitler, but the plan never came to fruition. Operation *Foxley* envisaged infiltrating a sniper team to kill Hitler at his home in Berchtesgaden. A German POW captured in Normandy had revealed Hitler took a stroll around 10:30 each morning and preferred his guards to keep their distance. The mission never went ahead. This may have been because the opportunity never arose, but by that stage in the war there were fears killing Hitler might turn him into a martyr figure. More pragmatically, there was the fear Hitler might be succeeded by a more competent military strategist. As a footnote to *Foxley*, SOE did come close to ending Hitler's life inadvertently. The July 1944 Stauffenberg plot saw German officers use captured SOE explosives and detonators in an attempt to assassinate Hitler in his Wolf's Lair headquarters in East Prussia. Only half the charges provided to the plotters were used, however, and Hitler survived the attempt.

The most famous single act of sabotage was against the Vemork Norsk Hydro plant in Norway. The possible use of nuclear weapons was already understood by the Allies and so preventing the Nazis from developing them first was a key strategic objective. An important part of the Nazi development programme was the manufacture of heavy water (deuterium oxide) at Vemork. In the early part of 1942 the

Allies learned the Germans were increasing output of this material. Due to the mountainous location of the plant, and the close proximity of Norwegian civilians, an air attack by

SWITCH NO. 10
(TIME PENCILS)
Catalogue No. A 1.

Switch No. 10 'time pencils'. These delayed-action fuses contained a corrosive liquid which dissolved a steel wire holding back a spring-loaded striker. (TNA HS 7/28)

bombers was initially discounted. Supplied with details of the guards and defences by Norwegian resisters, a commando attack by glider-borne engineer troops was considered the best means of attack. Prior to this, on 19 October 1942, a four-man team of SOE-trained Norwegians had been parachuted into the country. Known as Operation *Grouse*, this team was to prepare the way for the glider attack, which was codenamed Operation *Freshman*. After a gruelling trek on skis, *Grouse* arrived at the plant and made contact on 9 November. *Freshman* set off on 19 November. It was a complete disaster. The two gliders were towed by Halifax bombers, each containing two aircrew and fifteen soldiers. One of the bombers flew into a mountain with its glider crashing nearby. The other bomber tried to abort, but lost its glider in turbulence. The surviving commandos were captured, interrogated and shot under the terms of Hitler's notorious *Kommandobefehl* which ordered German forces to execute uniformed commandos without trial.

Despite this setback, SOE still had the original *Grouse* team in location. On the night of 16 February 1943 Operation *Gunnerside* saw an additional six Norwegian commandos parachuted in to support them. Following the failure of

The Norsk Hydro Plant at Vemork, which supplied Nazi scientists with heavy water required for atomic research. The plant was targeted by two SOE missions: *Freshman* and *Gunnerside*. (TNA HS 2/185)

Knut Haugland was a member of the Norwegian Independent Company commando team and was part of the team which sabotaged the heavy water plant at Vemork in 1943. (TNA HS 9/676/2)

Freshman the Germans had improved the defences of Vemork, planting additional mines and lighting around the plant. However, they discounted the possibility of an attack from the direction of a steep ravine and semi-frozen torrent. This was the route chosen, and the mission on the night of 27/28 February was a success, with production halted for several months. When production recommenced the plant was bombed by the United States Air Force (USAF), on 16 November 1943. Following the raid, the Germans decided to transfer all the surviving heavy water to Germany. This was reported to London by SOE agent Einar Skinnarland, who had played a vital role at every stage of the Vemork missions. On 20 February 1944 Knut Haukelid (one of the *Gunnerside* party) planted a bomb on a ferry steamer carrying the cargo and sank the ship and cargo in the middle of Lake Tinnsjø.

The ferry SF *Hydro*, which was sunk on 20 February 1944 in the middle of Lake Tinnsjø while carrying supplies of heavy water to be used in atomic research. (IWM HU 47396)

SOE IN THE BALKANS

AN EARLY FOCUS of SOE (and Section D before it) was Yugoslavia. This country offered access to the Romanian oilfields and contained strategically important copper mines, not to mention possibilities of blocking commercial traffic on the Danube. Yugoslavia was in a state of political turmoil at the time of the Nazi invasion in April 1941, with deep ethnic divisions between the various peoples who made up the country. SOE initially solicited aid from the Chetnik forces under the Serbian General Draža Mihailović. Unfortunately for SOE, Mihailović was less interested in fighting the Axis than he was in ensuring Serbian predominance in the post-war settlement, whichever side should emerge victorious.

Following the Nazi invasion of the Soviet Union on 22 June a new force rose to prominence in Yugoslavia. After the Nazi–Soviet nonaggression pact of 1939, the communist reaction to the European war was initially muted, with blame being levelled at the twin evils of capitalism and imperialism. However, when the Nazi *Blitzkrieg* thundered across the Soviet border the gloves really came off. Communist resisters across Europe were instructed to make direct attacks on Nazi forces regardless of the reprisals. Every hostage shot, they reasoned, would bring another family into the blood feud against Hitler's Germany. In Yugoslavia the communist partisans were led by General Josip Broz 'Tito'. Support from London for Tito was initially lukewarm; there was no particular desire to see Europe emerge from Nazi occupation only to see it embrace Soviet

domination. However, when Mihailović repeatedly failed to launch attacks against the Nazis, patience ran out. Churchill issued instructions to support Tito regardless of the long-term consequences. One of the most successful operations with Tito's forces was *Ratweek*, a series of coordinated attacks beginning on 1 September 1944 against Axis forces as they withdrew from the Balkans.

A radio operator in the field takes down a message received on his B2 wireless set at Mukaj, Albania in August 1944. (IWM HU 64885)

While its involvement in Yugoslavia was marked with frustration, SOE enjoyed more success in Greece. When the Allies were preparing for the Battle of El Alamein and the invasion of French North Africa (Operation *Torch*) in the autumn of 1942, SOE Cairo devised a scheme to interrupt the key German supply route to North Africa via Greece. At the time there was a single rail route from Central Europe to southern Greece and the port of Piraeus. Passing through mountainous terrain the railway's most vulnerable points were a series of three viaducts at Gorgopotamos, Asopos and Papadia. If one or more of these bridges were to be destroyed the supply line would be cut at a crucial moment in the war.

Codenamed Operation *Harling*, SOE's team of twelve was led by Colonel 'Eddie' Myers of the Royal Engineers and Major Chris Woodhouse. Myers had knowledge of demolition while Woodhouse, a classical scholar, was fluent in Greek and had some knowledge of the political situation in the country.

Resisters collect supplies dropped to them by Allied aircraft in France. Huge local effort was required to collect and transport supplies. (IWM HU 41895)

Harling parachuted into Greece on the night of 30 September. Myers scouted the three viaducts and selected Gorgopotamos as the target. The bridge was garrisoned by eighty Italians so the party required support from Greek

CONTAINERS, "H" TYPE

Catalogue No. 15C/170.

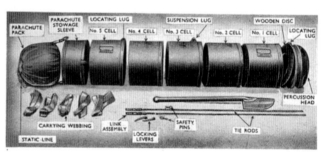

LAYOUT OF CONTAINER COMPONENTS

'H' Type containers were 5 feet 6 inches and 15 inches in diameter and broke into drums for ease of carrying. SOE dropped 76,504 containers with 10,000 tons of equipment, weapons and supplies. (TNA HS 7/28)

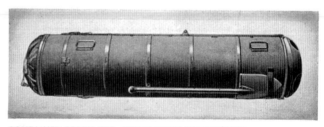

CONTAINER READY FOR ATTACHMENT TO AIRCRAFT

resistance fighters. The largest national resistance group was the EAM (National Liberation Front) and its paramilitary arm ELAS (Greek People's Liberation Army). EAM-ELAS was established by the Communist Party of Greece. The second largest group was the right-wing EDES (National Democratic Greek League) led by Colonel Napoleon Zervas. Needless to say there were complications trying to elicit support from both factions. It was not until 25 November that a force of 150 guerrillas was assembled to neutralise the Italian garrison in order for the demolition party to carry out its work. Even then, the mission did not quite go to plan.

'C' Type containers 5 feet 8 inches long and 15 inches in diameter. To prevent the contents being damaged, the base of the container had a percussion pad which crumpled on impact. (TNA HS 7/28)

The structure of the bridge was not what Myers had anticipated so the demolition team had to adapt their plastic explosive charges while a gun battle raged around them. By the early hours the bridge was extensively damaged and remained out of action for thirty-nine days.

Operation *Harling* was trumpeted as a major success by SOE. However, by the time the mission had been completed the Allied victory at El Alamein was already three weeks old, and Operation *Torch* had commenced on 8 November. Strategically the importance of the raid might be questioned. Less well known, but perhaps more successful, was Operation *Animals* in the summer

CONTAINERS, "C" TYPE

Catalogue No. ISC/65.   Jacob.
    „   „   ISC/120. White.

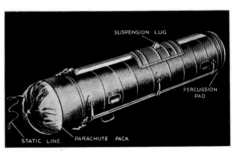

CONTAINER READY FOR ATTACHMENT TO AIRCRAFT

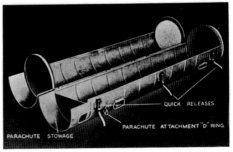

CONTAINER OPEN

Polish resister learning to assemble a gun blindfolded. SOE provided Poland's 'Home Army' resistance force with valuable assistance in training and supplies. (TNA HS 7/185/19)

of 1943. At this stage in the war the Allies were preparing Operation *Husky*, the invasion of Sicily on 10 July. The cover plan to *Husky* was codenamed *Barclay*, the purpose of which was to tie down Axis troops around the Mediterranean and keep them away from Sicily for as long as possible. Part of this deception included the famous Operation *Mincemeat*,

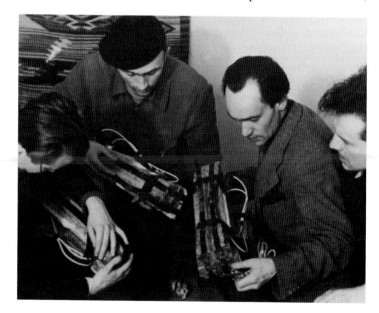

Polish resisters examining explosive charges prior to mining a railway bridge in April 1944. (TNA HS 7/185/29)

where fake documents were planted on a corpse washed up in Spain. While *Mincemeat* hinted the Allied invasion was aimed at Sardinia, *Animals* made it appear as if the invasion would come through Greece and the Balkans. Deception planners created a bogus Twelfth Army in the Eastern Mediterranean consisting of twelve divisions, none of which actually existed. SOE played its part in the deception by mounting around forty major attacks on the road and rail networks in Greece. As part of these attacks, Myers targeted the Asopos rail viaduct. Unable to elicit support from Greek resistance fighters for a direct attack on the German garrison, Myers sent a six-man team led by Captain Geoffrey Gordon-Creed. The party painstakingly climbed down an unguarded precipice and spent several days just a few hundred metres from the German garrison and its searchlights. On the night of 20 June the saboteurs went to work. When a German sentry nearly discovered the team, Gordon-Creed attacked the man with a cosh and threw him off the bridge into the gorge 100 metres below. The charges were successfully placed and the bridge remained out of action for three months. It was believed this attack resulted in the deployment of two German divisions to Greece, both of which could have been better used in Sicily.

One of SOE's more audacious coups was Major Patrick Leigh Fermor's kidnapping of General Heinrich Kreipe, Commander of the German 22nd Division on Crete. On the night of 26 April 1944 Fermor, his number two, Billy Moss and three Cretan resisters dressed in German uniforms flagged down Kreipe's staff car. The driver was neutralised and the general bundled onto the back seat. With Moss impersonating the driver, and Fermor wearing Kreipe's hat, the party drove through a succession of German checkpoints to the safety of a hideaway. On 14 May the SOE team were picked up by a British motorboat and taken to Egypt where Kreipe was interrogated.

THE ENGLAND GAME

THE 'DOUBLE CROSS System' stands alongside SOE and the work of the code breakers of Bletchley Park as one of the great British successes in the secret war. From 1940 onwards MI5 played a succession of double agents against the Nazis for the purpose of counterespionage and strategic deception.

Less well known, however, is the enormously successful German Operation *Nordpol* (North Pole), the playing back of captured SOE agents in the Netherlands. This was arguably SOE's greatest disaster and nearly led to the organisation being taken over by SIS. SOE's 'Plan for Holland' followed the typical strategy: the country would be divided into districts to which London would assign an organiser, an instructor and a radio operator. These would work with local resisters to build a secret army supplied from England and held in readiness until such time as it could coordinate its actions with Allied forces. In the meantime, to avoid exposing the population to reprisals, obvious sabotage attacks were discouraged. Of the fifty-six agents despatched between September 1941 and October 1943, forty-three fell into German hands on arrival and only eight survived until the end of the war. In addition to this, 544 containers of military stores were dropped and immediately fell into German hands. Not only that: eleven RAF aircraft were lost on operations delivering men and materiel through a heavily defended airspace. Something disastrous had clearly gone wrong.

Opposite: The Type A Mk. III transceiver suitcase radio was the smallest transceiver used by SOE. Marconi produced over 4,000 of these sets during the war. (IWM COM 229)

A radio operator in occupied France. Radio operators had to keep moving their hideouts lest Nazi detection services pinpoint their location. (IWM MH27378)

The problems for SOE began when informants in the Dutch resistance told the Germans of a supply drop on 27 February 1942. This supply drop was intercepted and the Germans began hunting for the wireless set which they deduced was being used to contact London. On 7 March the wireless operator Huub Lauwers was arrested in The Hague and taken in for questioning. The Head of Gestapo (secret police) in Holland was Joseph Schreieder. He joined forces with Hermann Giskes of the Abwehr (military intelligence) who conceived the idea of *Das Englandspiel* (the England Game), in other words running Lauwers as a double agent. Faced with execution, Lauwers agreed to transmit messages back to London on behalf of the Germans. Lauwers had been trained at Beaulieu to omit his secret identity check if captured so London would know he was operating under duress. Alas, in what appears to be a case of negligence rather than conspiracy, the Country Section ignored this breach in security protocols and continued to stay in contact with Lauwers, announcing the arrival of additional agents and supplies. Every time this occurred, Giskes organised a reception committee and had the agents arrested.

The first indication something was amiss was when the Country Section sent a Dutch radio operator a reminder to use his security checks, with the security check protocol added to the message. SOE's senior cryptographer, Leo Marks, queried this serious breach of security and was told not to worry by the Country Section, which claimed to have other ways of checking the agents were operating freely.

Marks was not satisfied by the answer and continued to have doubts about the Dutch operation. He then learned none of the Dutch radio operators had ever sent an incorrectly coded message. Under the strain of working behind enemy lines, all agents made mistakes when coding from time to time. Marks called these 'indecipherables'. The fact the Dutch messages were all perfectly enciphered indicated to Marks they were not made by agents, but probably by German cryptographers. To test this theory Marks sent an indecipherable of his own – something no field agent could possibly unravel. Sure enough a reply to the message was received. Separately to Marks one of the SOE radio operators also grew suspicious of the Dutch. Having sent a message to one of the Dutch radio sets, the British operator mischievously added the initials HH to the end of the message. This 'Heil Hitler' was a common sign-off used by German radio operators. Sure enough, there was an instantaneous HH transmitted in reply.

FANYs transcribing coded messages. With coding mistakes often made by agents in the field, coders could spend hours trying to break an 'indecipherable'. (IWM HU 47913)

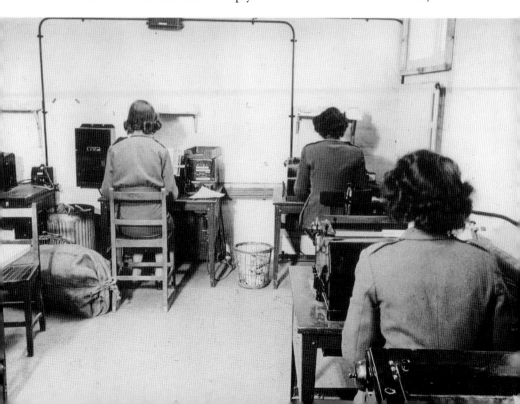

A cyanide capsule and container. Sucking an 'L' pill would normally kill within 30 seconds. Agents also had access to Benzedrine or amphetamines to overcome fatigue. (IWM EPH 10078)

These wine bottle corks have been adapted to conceal secret messages. (TNA HS 7/49)

The matter was referred to Gubbins, but however privately suspicious he might have been, he remained outwardly unconcerned. More Dutch agents were sent to their deaths. The deception was only finally acknowledged after the escape from Haaren concentration camp in August 1943 of two SOE agents, Pieter Dourlein and Johan Ubbink, codenamed *Sprout* and *Chive* respectively. Arriving in Switzerland, they

Corks. A normal cork as used in a wine bottle is used for the concealment of small codes and micro-prints. The cork has a hollow centre with a sliding panel.

revealed they had been arrested on arrival and had met other captured agents in prison. After this, there was a halt to SOE's Dutch operation. In order to give the captured agents some chance of survival, communication to the radio operators was maintained, but became very non-committal. At this point Giskes realised his deadly game had been uncovered. On 1 April 1944 he sent a message to London which ended '... whenever you will come to pay a visit to the Continent you may be assured that you will be received with the same care and result as all those you sent us before. So long.'

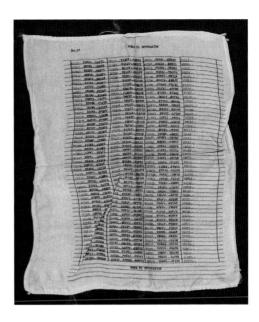

To replace vulnerable poem codes, SOE introduced 'worked out keys' (WOKs). Once used, the line of cipher was destroyed so an agent could not reveal his back traffic if captured. (IWM EPH 10088)

For decades after the war, many questioned if SOE had deliberately sent the Dutch agents to their deaths as part of some elaborate double bluff. It appeared inconceivable the section heads could have been guilty of nothing more than stupidity. The truth appears to be somewhere in the middle. Initially the Country Section had made genuine mistakes. However, in June 1943 SIS received reports that eight of the agents communicating with London had actually been arrested long before. The crisis caused by this revelation was used as a pretext by MI6 for taking control of SOE. At this time the planning for the Allied invasion of Europe had begun and Gubbins was fiercely guarding SOE's reputation and its right to exist. In order to protect the long-term viability of its operations, it appears Gubbins could not have afforded to highlight publicly his organisation's failings, no matter how serious they were. The cost of this was borne by the Dutch agents he continued to send in.

SOE IN FRANCE

WITH ITS CLOSE proximity to England, France was naturally the main focus of SOE's attention. Of course there was spontaneous resistance in France from many quarters; and from 1941 there was the communist resistance, the FTP. However, SOE's achievement was to coordinate and supply the resistance so it became an effective 'fourth arm' at the crucial moment. Four years on from the Dunkirk evacuation, on the eve of the Normandy landings, SOE was in touch with 137 active groups in France, with 100,000 armed men ready to take orders from London; not to mention a 'secret army' of another 350,000 men, 300,000 trade unionists and half a million railway workers willing to support the Allied cause. To these resisters, over 76,000 Sten guns had been supplied; 27,000 pistols, around 16,500 rifles, 3,000 Brens,

Contents of a captured supply container dropped to the French Resistance. The haul contains pistols, grenades, plastic explosive and also a spring-loaded cosh and commando knife (bottom right). (IWM HU 93138)

plus bazookas, mortars, antitank rifles, grenades, and high explosives. SOE's F Section alone had sent around 400 agents to help achieve this remarkable return.

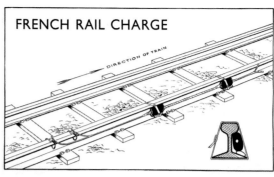

FRENCH RAIL CHARGE

The French rail charge, 1944. This comprised of two sets of explosives detonated by fog signals attached by cordtex. The charge normally destroyed one metre of track. (TNA HS 7/28)

While much of SOE's work was in identifying leaders of indigenous resistance and negotiating a political minefield of factions and personalities, there were a number of targeted 'in out' missions prior to D-Day. One of the first was Operation *Savannah*, an abortive attempt to kill German pathfinder bomber crews on their nights out. From inauspicious beginnings confidence in operating in France increased. Perhaps the most successful missions were those of the Gaullist RF Section's *Armada* team, led by *Marie* and *Goujon* (Raymond Basset and André Jarrot). Their first mission was to attack the power supplies to the Schneider-Creusot armament works in August 1943. After destroying a number of transformers and pylons, the team also destroyed stores of aviation fuel at Varennes-le-Grand. They returned to France in October the same year to attack the electricity supplies to Paris and the canal system which allowed the Germans to bring submarines and small craft from the North Sea to the Mediterranean. A third mission saw the team tasked with uniting the Maquis around Lyon in July 1944. *Marie* graduated from saboteur to leader of a group of 15,000 resisters. The *Armada* team's driver *Khodja* is also credited with killing eleven Gestapo officials in the Lyon area in the spring of 1944.

A more subtle approach to sabotage was favoured by the *Stockbroker* circuit organised by Harry Rée. In July 1943 two unsuccessful bombing missions had targeted the Peugeot tank turret factory at Sochaux. Rée contacted Rudolphe Peugeot and asked him for plans and access to sabotage the factory; if not, the RAF would return and more civilians would likely be injured. Peugeot was initially hesitant in responding to this blackmail – Rée could have been a Nazi stooge sent to test his loyalty. However, Rée arranged for the BBC to broadcast a message of Peugeot's choosing. The plant was put out of action for three months, and when replacement machinery did arrive, it was destroyed before it could be unloaded from the truck. Rée also tried to blackmail Michelin with the same terms, but was not successful. This time the bombers were called in.

The combined effect of innumerable sabotage operations had a sapping effect on German morale. Supplies sent by train would be redirected, railway turntables would be destroyed, plant and machinery would break down for no apparent reason. In the summer of 1943 a series of sabotage attack plans were drawn up by SOE. These would be activated to support an invasion, with the various regions called out by coded message broadcast by the BBC. These included Plan Green (attacks on railways), Plan Tortoise (attacks on reinforcements moving by road) and Plan Purple (dislocation of telecommunications). When the invasion came on 6 June 1944 the messages went out to the Resistance. In the Normandy area all the main telephone cables were put out

RF Section's 'Tommy' Yeo-Thomas helped organise resistance in France. He successfully lobbied Churchill to supply weapons to the Maquis, but was captured in Paris and sent to Buchenwald concentration camp.
(TNA HS 9/1458)

of action on or just after D-Day. The Germans attributed more rail cuts to saboteurs than Allied aircraft. One of the most telling impacts of resistance was the delaying by seventeen days of the arrival of 2nd SS Panzer Division Das Reich in the Normandy theatre. Based in Toulouse, this division was harried and obstructed by acts of sabotage and direct attacks as it crawled its way northwards.

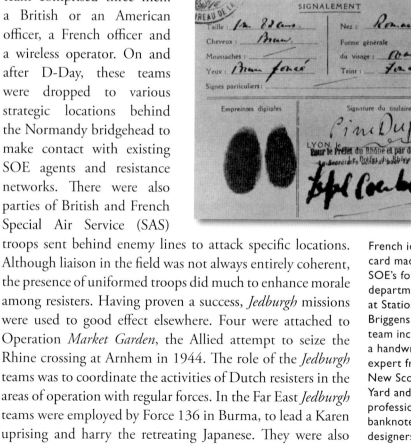

In order to coordinate resistance with the Allied command structure, SOE developed the *Jedburgh* scheme. Each *Jedburgh* team comprised three men: a British or an American officer, a French officer and a wireless operator. On and after D-Day, these teams were dropped to various strategic locations behind the Normandy bridgehead to make contact with existing SOE agents and resistance networks. There were also parties of British and French Special Air Service (SAS)

troops sent behind enemy lines to attack specific locations. Although liaison in the field was not always entirely coherent, the presence of uniformed troops did much to enhance morale among resisters. Having proven a success, *Jedburgh* missions were used to good effect elsewhere. Four were attached to Operation *Market Garden*, the Allied attempt to seize the Rhine crossing at Arnhem in 1944. The role of the *Jedburgh* teams was to coordinate the activities of Dutch resisters in the areas of operation with regular forces. In the Far East *Jedburgh* teams were employed by Force 136 in Burma, to lead a Karen uprising and harry the retreating Japanese. They were also used by the Free French in Indochina to good effect.

French identity card made by SOE's forgery department at Station XIV, Briggens. The team included a handwriting expert from New Scotland Yard and professional banknote designers. (TNA HS 7/49)

WOMEN IN SOE

AT ITS HEIGHT approximately one quarter of SOE's 13,000 personnel were women. The majority were drawn from the various Women's Services – the Auxiliary Territorial Service (ATS), Women's Auxiliary Air Force (WAAF), and the First Aid Nursing Yeomanry (FANY). Approximately 1,200 were directly employed civilians. The majority of women were employed in administration, as drivers, telephonists, or wireless operators and coders. Some were employed at SOE's London headquarters, and some in the various stations around the country. The majority were below the age of industrial and military conscription (i.e. under twenty). Often from privileged backgrounds, these young ladies were generally considered quick-witted, hardworking and saw their jobs as a privilege. It was well known that SOE girls were extremely security conscious and many never revealed their wartime role.

Perhaps the most important staff were the specialist radio operators and coders who maintained communications with agents in the field. Wireless operators were given four months' intensive training to bring them up to the speed of 125 letters per minute. Agents in the field would form their messages into groups of five coded letters, and it was vitally important the receiving operator accurately recorded the message first time to avoid keeping the field agent on the air for longer than necessary. Once they achieved the required speed they were posted to Grendon and Poundon where they worked six-hour

Opposite: SOE agent Jacqueline Nearn at firing range. This is a still from an information film called *Now It Can Be Told*. (IWM MH 24434)

shifts. At the beginning of the shift they would be given a list of the agents' call signs and their scheduled broadcast times, known as 'skeds'. There would then be a long vigil, waiting for one of their 'Joes' (as agents were known) to make contact. On occasion the messages were interrupted mid-signal, a sign the agent was in danger of discovery; or worse, had been killed at their radio set. Messages were sent to coders (cipher clerks) to be converted into clear text. Coders made it a point of honour to decipher messages which had become garbled in transmission, or incorrectly transcribed. They would spend hours attempting to break an 'indecipherable', often working long beyond their shifts. At its peak in the summer of 1944, SOE's stations in England were processing 300,000 'groups' a week (1.5 million individual characters). It was an epic undertaking.

One of the most secret roles played by women in SOE was to act as honeytraps for trainee agents at Beaulieu. The most notorious of these was *Fifi*, whose existence was believed to be a myth, but whose reality was confirmed in 2014. Hired as a 'special agent' in 1942 at the age of twenty-two, Marie Christine Chilver was of British and Latvian parentage; blonde, sophisticated, and fluent in French and German. Her modus operandi was to pose as a French journalist and be sent after agents who were on practice undercover missions. She would engineer an introduction, and then try to get the agent to reveal their true identity over dinner and drinks. Chilver would then report to the assessors at Beaulieu if the agent had been indiscreet or not. If the agent had revealed his mission, it would be the end of his career with SOE. The rumour *Fifi* would go to bed with the agents to see if they talked in their sleep is not upheld by her surviving reports.

A sergeant in headphones listens to Jacqueline Nearn practising Morse code. Every operator had a unique style, very much like hand-writing. This style was referred to as the 'fist'. (IWM MH 24440)

Of course, the most famous role of women in SOE was as secret agents, with forty-two female agents in F Section and another eleven in the Gaullist RF Section sent into occupied France. Although some did end up commanding large resistance groups, female agents were generally employed as wireless operators or couriers; young women were far less out of place in occupied Europe than young men of military conscription age. Unusually for women at the time, female

SOE's Clothing Shop. Stock-piles of clothes waiting to be issued to agents. Female agents were provided with bespoke garments. (TNA HS 7/49)

Working as a courier for SOE's *Jockey* circuit, in 1944 Polish-born Christine Granville (Krystyna Skarbek) bribed officials to have circuit organiser Francis Cammaerts released by the Gestapo. (TNA HS 9/612)

SOE agents were trained to fight, undertaking the same intense paramilitary training as the men. Behind enemy lines they might have to fight for their lives; something experienced by agent Nancy Wake who was forced to kill a German sentry with a hand chop to the throat on one of her many adventures.

The risk faced by radio operators was particularly high, with a life expectancy of six weeks. One of the many tragic cases was Noor Inayat Khan, a Russian-born, Indian noble with an American mother. She joined the WAAF in 1940 and trained as a wireless operator. Fluent in French, she was seconded to FANY and then recruited by SOE. While training as a secret agent Khan revealed it was against her religious principles to ever tell a lie. If captured on mission, an agent's ability to lie convincingly was their only real hope of salvation. With radio operators in desperate demand, Khan was flown by Lysander aircraft to France in June 1943. She travelled to Paris and remained at large until her betrayal four months later. Although she stubbornly resisted interrogation, Khan's notebooks were found containing her previous messages. This was a terrible breach of security on her part and allowed the Germans to play back her radio set to London, something which cost several other SOE agents their lives. On 25 November 1943 she escaped during an air raid but was quickly recaptured. Labelled as a *Nacht und Nebel* prisoner (lit. 'night and fog' – i.e. scheduled to disappear without trace), she spent the next ten months in solitary confinement, shackled in chains. On 11 September 1944 she was executed at Dachau with three other SOE prisoners: fellow radio operator Yolande Beekman, and couriers Eliane Plewman and Madeleine Damerment.

French-born Odette Sansom had married an Englishman and moved to Britain. In 1942 she was recruited to the FANY after responding to an appeal to provide family photographs and postcards of the French coast. She was landed near Cannes to act as a courier for the organiser of the *Spindle* circuit, Peter Churchill, who had been charged with supporting the Maquis in south-eastern France. The pair were captured in April 1943 and tortured. Their only hope of survival was to pretend that Churchill was a nephew of the British Prime Minister and that Odette was Peter's wife. Although sentenced to death and sent to Ravensbrück concentration camp, the plan worked. In a vain attempt to avoid the gallows, camp commandant Fritz Suhren actually drove Sansom over to the advancing Americans at the end of the war. The same Nazi had earlier overseen the executions of SOE agents Violette Szabo, Denise Bloch and Lilian Rolfe at the camp.

In addition to those despatched to France, there were several women recruited by SOE among the Jewish Parachutists of Mandate Palestine. These included Hannah Szenes, who was captured in Hungary and executed on 7 November 1944, and Sara Braverman, who evaded capture and went on to help establish the Israeli Defence Force Women's Corps. Haviva Reik took part in a mission to support an uprising in her native Slovakia against the Axis puppet government. When the Nazis stamped down on the uprising, Reik was captured and executed on 20 November 1944.

Radio operator Noor Inayat Khan was a British Muslim. Codenamed *Madeleine*, she was captured in Paris and later killed at Dachau. She was awarded the George Cross posthumously. (TNA HS 9/836/5)

POST WAR

As THE WAR in Europe drew to a close, it became increasingly apparent SOE would not survive the peacetime settlement. The only possible reason to keep SOE active was to subvert leftwing and communist parties in the recently liberated countries; but there was little stomach for that with Clement Attlee's Labour Party winning the General Election in July 1945. More tellingly, the Foreign Office signalled its unwillingness to have two peacetime secret agencies working abroad. On 15 January 1946 responsibility for sabotage and subversion therefore passed to SIS with the creation of a Special Operations Branch. Many personnel transferred over from SOE and served with MI6 during the Cold War era.

The sleeve gun fired a single .32-inch bullet with a range of 3 yards. It was designed to be fired point blank, pressed against the victim. (TNA HS 7/28)

There was one final piece of unfinished business performed at the war's end. Some captured agents had survived the concentration camps and returned home barely recognisable as their former selves. Many more remained unaccounted for. Gubbins wished to discover the fate of all the SOE agents who were still missing and so sent officers out to Europe to trawl through the extensive German records and interview staff from the camps. There were many unhappy endings to these missions.

A month after SOE ceased to exist, a fire in Baker Street destroyed many of SOE's records. Many have claimed the fire was deliberate. The surviving files were labelled 'secret' and are still in the process of being released. However, memory of the organisation lived on beyond the war years, and the heroism of its agents found their way into books and into films. In 1945 the Special Forces Club in Knightsbridge was

A demonstration of the sleeve gun reveals how effective it might be as a concealed weapon. Difficult to reload, it could also serve as a cosh. (IWM HU 56777)

A 'Welman' one-man submarine being transported for testing at Station IX. Four craft were used by the Norwegian navy in an unsuccessful attack on Bergen harbour in 1943. (IWM HU 56768)

founded for SOE veterans and resisters to come together and reminisce. Photographs of the agents still adorn the hallway and stairs today. The motto of the club is *Spirit of Resistance*, a fitting epitaph for the organisation. Arguments continue about the value of SOE and the true impact of its missions in the strategic sense; but if nothing else, the real value of the organisation was it showed the occupied nations they had not been forgotten, and that there was hope, even in those darkest days.

FURTHER READING

Boyce, F., & Everett, D. *SOE: The Scientific Secrets*. Sutton, 2003.

Buckmaster, Maurice. *Specially Employed*. Batchworth Press, 1952.

Cruickshank, Charles. *SOE in the Far East*. Oxford University Press, 1983.

Foot, M. R. D. *SOE in France, An Account of the Work of the British Special Operations Executive in France, 1940–1944*. Her Majesty's Stationery Office, 1966.

Foot, M. R. D. *The Special Operations Executive 1940–1946*. BBC Books, 1984.

Giskes, Hermann J. *London Calling North Pole*. Kimber, 1953.

Lorain, Pierre. *Secret Warfare: The Arms and Techniques of the Resistance*. Orbis, 1984.

Mackenzie, William. *The Secret History of SOE: Special Operations Executive 1940–1945*. St Ermin's Press, 2002.

Marks, Leo. *Between Silk and Cyanide: A Codemaker's War 1941–1945*. HarperCollins, 1999.

Mears, Ray. *The Real Heroes of Telemark: The True Story of the Secret Mission to Stop Hitler's Atomic Bomb*. Hodder & Stoughton, 2003.

Michel, Henri. *The Shadow War: European Resistance 1939–1945*. A. Deutsch, 1972.

Millar, George. *Maquis: The French Resistance at War*. William Heinemann, 1945.

Rigden, Denis. *SOE Syllabus: Lessons in Ungentlemanly Warfare, World War II*. Public Record Office, 2001.

Seaman, Mark. *Operation Foxley: The British Plan to Kill Hitler*. Public Record Office, 1998.

Seaman, Mark. *Secret Agent's Handbook of Special Devices: World War II*. Public Record Office, 2000.

Stafford, David. *Secret Agent: The True Story of the Special Operations Executive*. BBC Worldwide Ltd., 2000.

PLACES TO VISIT

Airborne & Special Operations Museum Foundation,
100 Bragg Blvd, Fayetteville, North Carolina 28301.
Telephone: 001 910 643 2778.
Website: www.asomf.org

Churchill War Rooms, Clive Steps, King Charles Street,
London SW1A 2AQ.
Telephone: 020 7930 6961.
Website: www.iwm.org.uk/visits/churchill-war-rooms

Combined Military Services Museum, Station Road,
Maldon, Essex CM9 4LQ.
Telephone: 01621 841826.
Website: www.cmsm.co.uk/collections.php

Imperial War Museum, Lambeth Road, London SE1 6HZ.
Telephone: 020 7416 5000.
Website: www.iwm.org.uk

The Land, Sea and Islands Centre, Arisaig PH39 4NJ.
Telephone: 01687 450771.
Website: www.road-to-the-isles.org.uk

The Military Intelligence Museum, Building 200,
Chicksands, Shefford, Bedfordshire SG17 5PR.
Telephone: 01462 752896.
Website: www.militaryintelligencemuseum.org

The National Archives, Kew, Richmond, Surrey TW9
4DU. Telephone: 020 8876 3444.
Website: www.nationalarchives.gov.uk

National Motor Museum, Beaulieu, New Forest,
Hampshire SO42 7ZN.
Telephone: 01590 612345.
Website: www.beaulieu.co.uk/attractions/secret-army-
exhibition

The National Museum of Computing, Block H, Bletchley
Park, Milton Keynes MK3 6EB.
Telephone: 01908 374708.
Website: www.tnmoc.org
Natural History Museum, Cromwell Road, London SW7
5BD.
Telephone 020 7942 5000.
Website:paulletters.com/natural-history-museum-in-
world-war-ii-unnatural-and-far-from-historical
Noor Inayat Khan Memorial Trust, 48 Beverley Gardens,
Wembley, Middlesex HA9 9QZ.
Telephone: 020 8904 2533.
Website: www.noormemorial.org
Violette Szabo GC Museum, Cartref, Tump
Lane, Wormelow, Herefordshire HR2 8HN.
Telephone: 01981 540 477.
Website: www.violette-szabo-museum.co.uk/foyer.htm

INDEX